101 Dating Questions

Dating Tips and Advices, Including Fun, Interesting and Ice Breaker Questions You Should Know

Heather Henderson

PUBLISHED BY:

Heather Henderson

TABLE OF CONTENTS

CHAPTER 1: DATING   4

What Is Dating?   4

The Purpose of Dating   5

CHAPTER 2: DATING BASICS: WHAT TO REMEMBER BEFORE YOUR DATE   7

The Dating Dos   7

The Dating Don'ts   12

101 QUESTIONS   15

CHAPTER 3: QUESTIONS TO BREAK THE ICE   15

CHAPTER 4: FUN AND INTERESTING QUESTIONS   27

CHAPTER 5: QUESTIONS THAT REVEAL YOUR DATE'S PASSIONS AND INTERESTS   38

CHAPTER 6: QUESTIONS TO GET TO KNOW YOUR DATE ON A PERSONAL LEVEL   44

CHAPTER 7: QUESTIONS THAT REVEAL YOUR DATE'S THOUGHTS ABOUT RELATIONSHIPS.   63

CHAPTER 8: QUESTIONS THAT REVEAL YOUR DATE'S THOUGHTS ON FAMILY AND MARRIAGE   77

Chapter 1: Dating

What Is Dating?

The term "dating" refers to the period of courtship in which two people that are romantically attracted and interested in each other embark on a series of dates, in order to get to know each other better.

Normally two people who decide to go on their first date together choose a public place to meet, such a cafe, coffee shop, movie theatre or restaurant.

One of the most popular options is for prospective daters to meet for dinner and a movie. Many people like the idea of seeing a movie on a first date as if it doesn't go well they don't necessarily have to try to keep a conversation going and can just relax and enjoy the film.

First dates tend to be short, in case the two people on a date don't get on or struggle to find something in common to talk about.

Some daters even set up an escape plan by organizing for a friend to ring them while they're out on a date. If the date isn't going well, they can pretend that they have an urgent emergency to attend to.

Traditionally the dating period ends once two people decide they want to be exclusive and become boyfriend and girlfriend.

If two people that are dating find there is no chemistry between them or that they are better suited as friends, the dating period or courtship will also end.

If both parties are mature and responsible a relationship can end amicably. However in some cases where one or both parties feel they have been hard done by, lied to or cheated on, such an amicable split may not be possible.

The Purpose of Dating

The main purpose of dating is to see whether two people are compatible which each other. The second purpose of dating is to ascertain whether or not two people could share a future together.

Although two people may be physically attracted to each other, there is always the possibility that they won't make suitable partners. The dating process is designed to assess whether or not two people would make suitable life partners.

As an example, two people may find they are incompatible as their personalities clash, or they have contrasting religious, cultural, political or moral views and beliefs.

Of course dating is also a great way to ascertain whether two people have chemistry together or not. For a relationship to be successful both parties should be attracted to each other.

Without attraction it's impossible for a couple to share chemistry. Some people argue that chemistry and attraction is what makes a close friendship different to a romantic relationship.

Although it will normally take a few dates for a couple to decide whether or not they should continue with their relationship. It normally only takes people one date or a few minutes to ascertain whether or not they share chemistry.

The term chemistry refers to the spark two people feel who are attracted to each other. Chemistry isn't something tangible, or something that you can see. Rather it describes whether or not two people click or are drawn together.

Normally first dates are casual and neither party feels obligated to go on a second date, if they don't enjoy themselves. People have different opinions on when two people officially become a couple.

Some people put forward the notion that when you begin to date someone, you become a couple, while others argue that people can go on multiple dates, with multiple people and a pair only become a couple when they agree to call each other boyfriend and girlfriend.

However most people will agree that they don't automatically become boyfriend and girlfriend on a first date.

While first dates can be intimidating, they don't have to be. In fact first dates can even be pleasurable if you know how to initiate and maintain a natural conversation and make your date feel at ease.

Chapter 2: Dating Basics: What to Remember before Your Date

The Dating Dos

Preparation is paramount if you want to impress your date and perhaps even set up a second date. If you follow the basic dating rules, you'll have a much greater chance of impressing your date.

Be on time

First impressions are crucial, if you're late, you may give your date the impression that you will be late on future dates and that you might not be a reliable person.

By being on time you also show basic courtesy and that you acknowledge and value your date's time.

After all your date could very well be giving up a fun night with their friends, in order to meet you.

By showing up on time you also show that you're excited about the date and that you're genuinely interested in getting to know your date.

Be Yourself

Trust that you are an interesting person. As an example, don't try too hard to be funny, if you're not a naturally humorous person.

Also don't fake an interest in a topic you're not really interested in, or you don't know nothing about. If you're not interested in a subject simply subtly change the conversation to something you are interested in discussing.

As an example if you haven't set foot in a book store or a library in years, don't pretend that you're a book lover, as you might get caught out if you're asked a question that you don't know the answer to.

Instead of worrying about the things you're not, or don't know about, why not tell your date about all the things that you're genuinely interested in or passionate about.

If you're passionate about something you'll be interesting. Even if you just talk about your job, family or hobbies, you'll be interesting to your date.

You have to remember that everything you reveal to your date will be new knowledge to them, as they are just getting to know you.

Although your close friends may well be sick of hearing the same old stories your date would probably love nothing more than to hear you share your favorite stories and memories.

Be Friendly and Happy

One of the most important things to remember on a date is to be friendly and to enjoy yourself.

People, who are friendly and sociable, are instantly more attractive than people who are grumpy, or who make it clear that they aren't enjoying themselves and would rather be elsewhere.

After all, would you go on a second date with someone who looked grumpy or bored throughout the duration of your first date? Your answer is likely, no.

If you don't want to go on a date, then politely cancel. There is no point wasting someone else's time if you're no longer interested.

Just think about how you'd feel if you made a lot of effort to dress up for a date and then you realized that your date was no longer romantically interested in you. You'll probably feel embarrassed and rejected.

Listen to Your Date

Make sure that you really listen to what your date is saying. An outstanding date will have the knack of making sure the person they are dating feels like they are the only person in the room.

When you're on a date your mind should never be anywhere else. Next time you're out on a date make an effort to temporarily put aside thoughts about what's going on at the office, or what you're doing in the weekend.

When you're on a date it's of the utmost importance to be fully present. When you're fully present on a date, you'll be able to make the most out of the experience and make a great first impression on your date.

A great way of letting your date know your listening to them is by asking them friendly questions on the topic they are talking about.

Also try nodding periodically, this gesture will indicate to your date that you're paying close attention to what they're saying.

So as an example, if your date talks to you about their recent holiday, perhaps ask them about their favorite attraction or tourist activity. You might even learn some useful information in the process.

Show Genuine Interest in Your Date

Try to find subjects that both you and your date are interested in and be sure to ask open ended questions to keep the conversation going.

After all, the more effort you put into keeping your conversation going the more effort your date is likely to make in return.

Also make sure not to talk at length about an obscure interest, as it may bore your date. After all not everybody shares the same interests.

As an example if you're a comic book collector or a keen gardener, it's alright to tell your date about your interest but don't spend half the date talking about it, unless your date seems really enthusiastic about what you have to say.

Never ask questions that can be simply answered with a yes or no response, as you'll never get a conversation started with these sorts of open ended questions.

Try to get more information about your date so you can make an interesting conversation with him/her based on his/her interests

If you listen carefully to your date, you'll be able to get to know what their interests are. This information can be useful, so that you can tailor conversations and dates to his or her interests.

As an example if you find out that your date loves dancing, then perhaps take him or her to a dance class on a future date.

Most people will be extremely impressed if you remember the little details and listen carefully to what they say.

Also if your date is particularly comfortable talking about a certain subject make sure to ask them follow up questions which are related to the same subject.

Be Attentive to Your Date

Be sure to make sure that your date is happy and comfortable.

As an example if you're date mentions that they aren't a seafood fan and you've taken them to a seafood restaurant offer to take them somewhere else.

Make sure your date knows that you care about how they feel and are more than willing to cater to their needs.

If you're male and you're on an outdoor date make sure to offer your date your jacket if you sense that they're cold. Chivalry isn't dead and simple gestures like this can show your date how attentive and gentleman you are.

If you're female there is no reason why you can't open a door for your date too. Most men would appreciate such a gesture.

Make Eye Contact

During your date it's extremely important to maintain eye contact with your date. Eye contact creates a connection and shows your date that you're interested in what they have to say.

Studies also show that people who are reluctant to show eye contact often aren't confident or have something to hide. Most people for example, won't make eye contact when they are lying or being dishonest.

Proper eye contact is an art form, make sure not to stare at or eye ball your date. Instead keep a natural friendly eye contact and shift your glance occasionally.

After all the intention of maintaining an eye contact isn't to make your date feel uncomfortable but to create and maintain a connection.

Also take into consideration the fact that someone may be uncomfortable making eye contact, due to their cultural upbringing. In some cultures looking someone in the eyes is seen as a mark of disrespect.

However, in most western countries there is nothing rude about making eye contact. So don't put off making eye contact.

The Dating Don'ts

Don't Leave Your Phone On

It's extremely rude to answer your mobile phone, while you are out on a date.

The only exception is when there is an emergency, for example if you have children at home who may need to contact you, or you have a family member in the hospital.

If this is the case be sure to let your date know upon your arrival about the circumstance. By letting your date know that you have to keep your phone turned on during their date, from the onset they are more likely to understand should you need to take a phone call during your date.

If you don't have a good reason to keep you phone turned on simply switch your phone off when you arrive at the venue of your date.

This simple action will demonstrate to your date that they have your full and undivided attention.

Also try your best to refrain from sending text messages. If your date catches you texting they make think you'd rather be with the person who you are texting, than on the date with them.

Texting during a date is just as rude as making a phone call. If in doubt just turn your phone off, it's that simple.

Never Pretend to Be Someone You Aren't

If someone doesn't like you for who you really are, then they certainly aren't worth dating.

If you come across as genuine and honest, you are more likely to impress your date, than if you make up lies to impress them. Human beings are much for adept at recognizing lies than you may realize.

Also make sure never to lie before your first date. So many people, who meet their dates online, feel the need to lie about everything from their physical appearance to their age and career.

Don't kid yourself if you lie about yourself prior to meeting your date, there is absolutely no chance that your date will be willing to date you.

So do yourself a huge favour and be honest with your date from the time which you first make contact with them. This way you won't waste your time or your date's time.

Don't Monopolize the Conversation

Ideally a conversation should flow evenly between two people.

Although it's important to tell your date about yourself, so they get to know you, it's also important to show them that you're interested in what they have to say.

No one wants to go on a date with someone who is self-obsessed and just wants to talk about themselves.

If you're the type of person who likes the sound of your own voice, you need to realize that a date is about two people.

By monopolizing a conversation, you'll indicate to your date, that you're not actually interested in them at all. Your date may even think that you just want an audience to ramble on to.

If you want to talk endlessly about yourself, a date is not the right scenario to do so.

Don't Mention Your Ex or Your Last Date

So many people make the mistake of mentioning an ex or multiple ex partners on their first date.

The honest truth is that no one wants to hear about their dates' exes on a first date. In fact most people would feel awkward and uncomfortable in such a situation.

Just because a date doesn't protest or tell you to stop talking about your ex, doesn't mean that they're enjoying the conversation.

The danger in doing so is that you may give your date the impression that you still harbor feelings for your ex, or even worse that your still in love with your ex.

If you're still in love with your ex, you really shouldn't be dating anyone, until you're ready to move on from your ex emotionally.

Your ex is your ex for a reason, leave them in the past. After all, if you want to meet the love of your life, you'll never do so, while you're still pining for your ex-boyfriend or girlfriend.

101 Questions

Chapter 3: Questions to Break the Ice

1. What are your Saturdays like?

By asking your date about how they spend their Saturdays, you're likely to find out some useful information about their personality.

This information may give you an insight into whether your lifestyle matches theirs, or if you're likely to have disagreements on how to spend your free time should you decide to continue dating.

As an example, if they tell you they often work on Saturdays, there is a large chance that they might be a workaholic.

Or if they tell you they play sport with a team on Saturdays it may mean they are athletic, lead a healthy lifestyle and get on well with others.

How someone spends their free time tells us a lot about their personality and lifestyle. So remember to pay attention.

2. Do you have a nickname and if so is there a story behind it?

Asking your date about their nickname is a great ice breaker as normally people have funny stories to share on how they earned their nickname.

Nicknames are also very personal and if your date feels comfortable sharing their nickname with you they'll start to feel more comfortable sharing intimate details about their life with you.

Talking about nicknames is a great way to bond with your date. If you decide to continue dating your date, you might one day get the chance to give them a special pet name or nickname. As many couples refer to each other by special nick names.

3. Did you go to college/university? If so what subjects did you major in?

This question can lead to further discussion about what college your date attended, whether they stayed in a dorm with a roommate, were a member of a sorority or fraternity, studied abroad for a year or joined any clubs.

If you attended college yourself you'll also be able to bond with your date over sharing stories from your college years. Perhaps you'll be able to share stories about the activities you joined or friends you made.

Asking your date about the subjects they majored in can be a great idea as their answer will give you an idea about the sorts of subjects they find interesting and the types of careers they may be interested in pursuing in the future.

If your date answers that they haven't been to university, make sure not to seem disappointed or make them feel embarrassed.

There isn't anything wrong with not having been to college and it's never too late to enroll. In fact enrolling into a university as a mature student might even be an advantage as mature students are likely to have more work and life experience.

In fact some multimillionaires like the late Steve Jobs and Bill Gates dropped out of college. So make sure not to judge a book by its cover, just because you're date didn't attend college, or dropped out, doesn't mean that they won't become successful.

If your date didn't attend university perhaps go on and ask them about their high school experiences instead! Perhaps you can ask your date about their favorite high school subjects and teachers.

4. Who was your most inspiring college professor and why?

This is a great question to ask instead of asking who their favorite professor is as students often choose the most easy-going and relaxed professors as their favorites.

There is also always a chance that your date's favorite professor wasn't necessarily the professor who had the biggest impact on their studies and their life.

What is more interesting however is by finding out what inspires your date you'll also discover what motivates them in life and what they are passionate about.

Perhaps your date is inspired by making innovative new discoveries in their chosen field of study.

5. What would you do if you won a million dollars?

This question will reveal your date's inner most desires as well as some of their personality traits. This question is also a fun question to ask, as although not everyone will admit it.

Most people will day dream occasionally about what they'd do if they were lucky enough to win the lottery.

As an example, this question should reveal if your date is financially responsible and educated. If your date tells you they would spend their million dollars on flash cars for example this could be a warning that they aren't wise with their money.

It's never a wise idea to go out with someone who isn't financially responsible as their debt can easily become your debt, especially if you get married.

If however your date tells you they would splash out on a trip to Europe but would invest and save the rest then you should be rest assured that your date is financially responsible.

If you do come into a large sum of money, you have to be wise about how you manage it. Statistics show that over half of those who win lottery prizes of over one million dollars blow the entire sum within a few short years.

6. If you could live in any country in the world, which country would you pick?

This is a fun question that your date should enjoy answering.

It's important to mix fun questions in with your more serious questions, so that you date doesn't feel like they are in a job interview or being interrogated. After all if your date feels as if they're being interrogated, they're not likely to agree to go on another date with you.

The number one rule in going out on dates is that at their core they are meant to be fun. A fun date is normally a successful date. If you look like you're having fun and you've managed to put a smile on your dates face, you're on the right track.

After all would you be likely to go on a second date with someone if you didn't have a good time? Your answer is probably, no.

This question should also give you an indication on whether or not your date is a keen international traveler. Some people have the travel bug and start planning their next trip, the moment they get back from an overseas trip.

If your date answers quickly that they would pick their own country they may well be the type of person who feels more comfortable with what is familiar than exploring new things.

They probably also wouldn't be too keen on learning a new language or trying authentic spicy ethnic food. So if you're quite adventurous, make sure that you find a date who shares your excitement for trying new things.

However if you don't have the travel bug, your date picking your own country could be an indication that you're compatible when it comes to wanting to put down roots in your own country.

So for some people the fact that there date isn't particularly adventurous, when it comes to travel, might not be a bad thing.

After all if you're not keen on travel you probably wouldn't want to be in a long term relationship with someone who wants to move from one country to another every few years. As it would mean that you'd have to sacrifice important parts of your life to travel with your partner, or that you'd have to enter a long distance relationship.

Of course if you love travel, look out for dates who are interested in travelling to some of the countries you have on your bucket list. Many happy couples claim that there is no better way to travel than with a romantic partner.

7. What is your favorite book and why?

Firstly, this question will reveal whether or not your date enjoys reading.

While their answer may not be a deal breaker, it may give you an indication on whether or not they are an intellectual and a deep thinker.

Most intellectuals love reading and discovering new ideas as well as challenging and reforming their own ideas.

On the flipside people who aren't keen on reading, are often are outgoing and enjoy socializing. Of course avid readers can be extroverted too.

It pays never to judge a book by its cover as there is always an exception to every rule. It is possible after all to be a bookworm who also enjoys partying.

Also if you make assumptions about people, they're likely to get annoyed with you if you're wrong. Although most people stereotype other people, they don't handle being stereotyped themselves, well.

The book your date chooses will also tell you a lot about them. As an example if your date chooses a popular chick lit novel it's safe to say they are romantic, love pop culture and enjoy reading on a casual basis, while if your date chooses Leo Tolstoy's "War & Peace" they are likely to be more serious and more avid a reader.

If you and your date share a love of reading you might be able to swap book suggestions and discuss your favorite books over a casual cup of coffee in the future.

Remember, if you're enjoying your date, always be on the lookout for possible ideas for a future date. If you do, next time a date asks you what you'd like to do on your next date, you'll have a response ready.

Believe it or not most people would rather date someone who puts forwards ideas than someone who always leaves decisions up to other people.

8. What's the one movie you'll never grow tired of and could watch over and over?

This question is a great way of finding out what genres of movies your date likes to watch. Although of course there are some people who don't enjoy movies at all and enjoy spending time outdoors, listening to the radio or reading instead.

It's a great idea to remember the genre of movie that your date picks; as if the date goes well in the future you could invite your date out to see another movie of this genre.

As an example if your date enjoys Sci Fi and a new Sci Fi film is released by Steven Spielberg, why not invite your date out to a night at the movies. Popcorn included of course.

It's also favorable if your date picks a movie that you enjoy as couples who enjoy the same movies will have another common interest to talk about.

If you enjoy the same movies, you'll never have to worry about having to go to a movie alone again, because your friends share a different taste in movies compared to you.

After all if your date is obsessed with Sci Fi and you can't stand it, you'll often get bored when your date insists on rambling about it to you.

9. Do you have pets, if so what types?

If you're an animal lover you'll be more compatible with someone else who shares your love of animals.

If your date confirms that they do have a pet or pets then you'll have the opportunity to ask further questions. This question is a great ice breaker, as most pet owners will relish the chance to talk about their pets.

If you're not keen on animals then you'll be better off dating someone who doesn't have a pet. After all someone who is obsessed with cats will have a hard time living with someone who loathes them or that is allergic to them.

The type of animal someone has and its breed might also give you a clue about their personality. As an example someone who owns a large Labrador is likely to be an outdoorsy type who likes to keep active.

Also take into account that just because someone doesn't currently own a pet, doesn't necessarily mean that they don't like animals.

Some people love animals but due to their lifestyle or circumstances are unable to have one at the time being.

As an example if your date travels often, they probably are unable to keep a pet, as it would be unfair to the pet to be left at home for long periods of time.

10. Do you believe that everyone has a soul mate?

This question is perhaps one of the most important questions you can ask a new date, as their answer will indicate their general feeling about love and relationships.

Some people believe there are lots of people that they potentially could be compatible and happy with, while others believe that there is only one person they are meant to be with.

If you believe in soul mates you'll probably want to date someone who shares your belief.

While similarly if you believe there is more than one person who could share a happy life with, then you'll also be better off paired with someone who shares this belief.

11. Which genres of music do you enjoy?

Not only will this question tell you what genres of music your date likes, but it should give you an indication of how varied your dates other interests are likely to be.

As an example if your date tells you they enjoy a wide variety of music including country, pop, rap, classical and techno it is likely that they have a diverse range of contrasting interests.

While if your date answers that they only enjoy one genre of music they are likely to have a limited range of interests.

A date that has a wide range of interests is more likely to remain interesting in the long run, as you won't run out of thing to talk about.

Again it's preferable for your date to share some of your taste in music as couples who have more in common with each other are likely to get on better than couples who don't share any interests.

If you share a favorite band with a date why not organize to see them perform live if they visit your city?

After all most people appreciate surprises and who wouldn't enjoy seeing their favorite band perform live!

Just make sure to ask their friends and family whether they've brought tickets for the show or not, as you don't want to make the mistake of buying tickets, when they already have some.

Also if your date comments that they are a fan of a genre that you haven't really heard before, why not ask them to recommend one of their favorite songs from that genre?

After all, how do you know that you don't like a certain genre of music, if you've never really listened to it before?

12. What is the best piece of advice you've ever been given?

This is a question that you may actually take away some useful advice from, that you may be able to implement in your own life.

Why not tell your date in exchange a story about the best piece of advice you've ever been given. You never know, your advice might be particularly useful to your date.

This question may also give you an indication of the person or people who your date respects and is inspired by.

As an example, your date may well answer that their parents or grandparents gave them the best advice they've ever been given.

This would indicate that they are close with their family. If you're a family person this could be particularly good news.

13. If you could be any animal, which animal would you choose?

This question is a fun question that works particularly well as an ice breaker. The animal your date chooses may reflect their personality and or interests.

As an example someone who chooses a dolphin may enjoy swimming, while someone who chooses a dog may be loyal and affectionate.

This question may also provide an opportunity for some light hearted laughs as you and your date try to justify your decisions.

14. What sports are you interested in?

If you enjoy watching sports as a spectator or playing sports, either on your own or in a team, you may want to find a partner who shares your love of sports.

After all if you pride yourself on leading an active, sporty lifestyle you'll probably be incompatible with someone who doesn't exercise and prefers to spend their weekends on their couch.

Asking your date about sports can also lead to discussions on your favorite sports teams, players and sports tournaments.

If a major sporting tournament is taking place around the time of your date it could be a great idea to bring it up in discussion as most people follow major sports events such as the Olympics and it's a noninvasive topic to talk about on a first date.

Be careful though not to make the mistake of assuming that your date enjoys or watches sports. There are a large percentage of people, from all backgrounds, who don't enjoy watching or playing sports.

If your date isn't interested in talking about sports, then find another topic to talk about, or else you're guaranteed to bore your date. This rule applies to any topic you talk about. If your date doesn't seem interested, then simply switch topics.

15. What is your idea of a romantic evening?

It's of paramount importance that prospective dates share the same ideas on romance.

After all if you're idea of the perfect date entails a home cooked meal and a night curled up on the couch with your boyfriend or girlfriend, you probably won't want to date someone who wants to dance the night away every night.

Although it's important to take in to consideration that some people might want a partner who is different to them in order to calm them down or take them out of their shell.

By asking your date about their idea of a romantic evening you'll be able to assess whether or not romance would flourish between the two of you.

If you're an old fashioned romantic at heart you'll obviously want to date someone who enjoys romantic surprises such as receiving heart shaped chocolates or a love note on their pillow on occasion.

16. If you could live in your dream home, what would it look like?

Your date's dream home may tell you a lot about their dream lifestyle. While some people will choose a multimillion dollar mansion, others will choose a homey cozy cottage and others a flash modern city apartment.

Your date's choice in dream home will also give you an indication of the things they value most in life.

As an example some people will mention large family areas, this may indicate that they value a happy family life, first and foremost.

If your date tells you they would have a walk in wardrobe, this may indicate that they are somewhat materialistic and covet designer threads.

Chapter 4: Fun and Interesting Questions

17. When did you last laugh so much it hurt?

You know something is truly hilarious when you laugh so much that your stomach hurts.

Most people will have a funny story about the last time they laughed this hard that they're more than willing to share.

If you laugh at your date's story, you'll also score brownie points as when people laugh together, they grow more comfortable and feel as if they're bonding.

18. Where is your favorite place in the world?

The answer your date gives will tell you where they feel most content and happy.

As an example if your date's favorite place in the world is their family home, this may suggest that their family, comfort and security are important to them.

If your date chooses a tranquil spot outdoors as their favorite place in the world, they might value an active healthy lifestyle and spending time outdoors.

19. If you were given a free ticket to anywhere in the world, which destination would you pick?

So many people have a list of countries which they would love to visit, but haven't yet had the opportunity to.

This question is a fun question to ask; as it takes away all the constraints that everyday life puts in the way of travel and lets your date pick any destination in the world.

After all it's not often that people ask each other questions without restraints. Being able to think without constraints can actually be quite liberating.

Although this question is intended first and foremost to be a fun question, your dates answer will still give you an insight into their personality.

As an example if your date chooses a city that is a popular tourist destination, they may well like to follow the crowd, so to speak.

Whereas if your date chooses a destination you've never even heard of, they are likely to have the personality of an adventurer.

20. How do you like to spend your spare time?

This question should reveal whether your date prefers to spend their free time relaxing at home, pursuing hobbies or socializing.

Your dates answer may also give you an idea of how much time your date might have to spend with you in the future, should you choose to enter a long term relationship.

As an example if your date pursues a different hobby each night of the week, they may have little time left to spend with you. However, a date that has no hobbies or interests may be lazy or a bore in the long run.

So it's probably best to date someone who has a few hobbies but still has a few nights a week to spend with you.

21. If you were marooned on a desert island, what three objects would you choose to help you survive or escape?

We've all heard this question before, but it's useful anyhow, to gain an insight into your date's personality, without having to ask obvious or tedious questions.

Some people will take a serious logical approach to this question and will choose items that will help them survive or escape.

Examples of such items include a first aid kit, a radio transmitter and a tool box.

People who take a logical approach to this question are more likely to take a logical approach to the obstacles that they face in life. If you date a logical person, they are more likely to be reliable and steadfast.

Other people will take a more light hearted approach to this question and may choose items which will allow them to have more fun on their island.

Examples of such items include an elaborate tree house, an iPod, a book or a toilet. Some people will even choose their celebrity crush.

People who take a light hearted approach to this question are more likely to be light hearted and carefree in real life.

Lighthearted people can be fun to date, as long as they know when and where it's important to take a logical approach.

22. Would you rather live by the seaside or on a mountain?

This fun question should reveal whether your date prefers a warm or cold climate.

If your date picks the seaside it is likely that they prefer summer and days spent swimming and lounging around the beach. If your date chooses the mountain option they might prefer winters spent skiing or snowboarding.

It's preferable that your date chooses the same answer you do as if you get into a serious relationship later down the track you'll easily be able to plan vacations together.

After all if you want to travel to Aspen for a week on the slopes and your date would rather spend a week in Florida, you might have a problem.

Of course you could always compromise but wouldn't it be ideal to share similar tastes in vacations with your significant other?

23. If you could have any superpower, what would it be?

In recent years superheroes have become part of mainstream pop culture, thanks to a slew of blockbuster superhero movies being released.

Let's face it; there aren't many people who would turn down the opportunity to be granted a super power. So why not ask your date about which power they would select, if given the choice?

This question should reveal your dates inner most desires. As an example if someone chooses mind control then they might well be controlling and domineering in real life.

Your dates chosen super power may also show you how original and creative they are. Some people choose a traditional superpower, such as the ability to fly, invisibility or super strength, while in comparison others will make up their own unique super power such as the ability to influence other people's dreams.

24. What are some of the craziest things you've done?

This question is a great way to find out whether or not your date is too wild for your taste.

As an example if you prefer to obey rules and your date reveals that they engaged in dangerous illegal activities you may decide there and then not to go on a second date.

However if some of the activities your date listed sound like fun, then you may have met your match. If your date is interested in the same crazy activities that you enjoy, why not consider taking on a new challenge together?

Some possible adventurous ideas to consider include bungee jumping, sky diving, swimming with the sharks and mountain climbing.

25. Who is your celebrity crush?

When you ask this question, keep your fingers crossed that your date chooses a celebrity that you resemble slightly or that you share distinct personality traits with.

However don't be put off if you are brunette and your date picks a blonde, or vice versa, as you can't be certain your date picked the celebrity based on their hair color.

Also try and remember your dates answer to this question as it may help you score brownie points with your date later down the track, should you choose to continue dating.

As an example if your date tells you that they have a crush on an actor or actress, why not take them on a date to the movies to see their crushes' latest film?

26. Which celebrity would be your dream date?

You may well find that the celebrity your date choose as their crush, wouldn't be their dream date.

After all while some attractive celebrities may make suitable crushes, their personalities or habits may rule them out from being date material.

This question is meant to be lighthearted and a great ice breaker. If you want you can also ask your date other questions, such as where the dream date would take place and what would be on the menu.

Planning out your dream date scenario with your date can be fun, so make sure to play along and share your dream date. Bonus points if your celebrity crush bears a resemblance to your date.

Who knows, perhaps they'll remember some of the details you shared with them and will incorporate them into a future date.

27. What is the stupidest question you've ever been asked?

This question is bound to result in a few shared laughs and laughing is a great way to bond with a new date. People instantly feel more comfortable around people they've shared a chuckle with.

Perhaps turn this question into a game and see which of you has been asked the stupidest question. Perhaps someone asked you if Paris was a country or if it were possible to drive from Australia to New Zealand?

A little tip though, if you suspect that your date is a few sandwiches short of a picnic, refrain from asking this question as they probably won't be able to relate to the feeling of irritation one experiences when being asked a stupid question, as they probably are one of the people who goes around asking such ridiculously stupid questions.

28. What was the worst thing you can remember doing as a kid?

Even adults who were angelic as children can remember doing something they weren't allowed to. We're all human and sometimes even those with the highest morals slip up.

Perhaps your date will reveal that they drew on their siblings face with a permanent marker while they were sleeping or that they cheated on a test.

Hopefully your date doesn't admit to any serious misdemeanors. After all no one could blame you if you thought twice about continuing to date someone, who openly admitted that they stole on a regular basis or took hard drugs as a child.

There is also the chance, that if you're date committed crimes as a child that they are still committing the crime, as committing crime can become a habit.

If your date shows remorse while sharing their story, this demonstrate that they try to lead a fair and honest life.

If your date doesn't show any regret they may still enjoy engaging in behavior that has negative consequences that hurts other people.

29. If you were a famous actor, what roles would you audition for?

Although not everyone would admit it, most people would jump at the chance to become a famous actor or actress.

So why not ask your date about the dream roles they would audition for, if only they were a famous Hollywood actor?

Your date's choice of genre should give you a few clues about their personality. As an example if your date reveals that they'd love to star in a romantic comedy, they are probably an old fashioned romantic at heart.

If however your date reveals that they'd love to be in a serious Oscar winning drama, it's likely that they have a serious personality and have an urge to be taken seriously and respected by others.

Most genres will give you some information about your date's personality. If your date mentions that they love period dramas, they're probably a history buff and if your date chooses a screen adaptation of a book, it's pretty safe to assume that they're an avid reader.

If you get the impression that your date enjoyed this question why not ask them what movie they would cast you in?

This is a great question to reveal how your date really sees you. Sometimes people are so caught up in their own perception of themselves that they're not aware of how other people really see them.

Don't take the movie your date chooses for you too seriously, as you can't really be sure of why and what made them chose it.

As an example, don't despair if your date picks a horror or thriller as most likely they don't think you look like a monster.

Perhaps your date sees you as a hot tough girl or guy who can handle a horror villain with your eyes closed.

30. What do I have to do to get a second date with you?

Remember only to use this question if you're genuinely interested in going on a second date.

After all, if you're not interested, you won't want to give your date the wrong impression. Otherwise you may receive phone calls, emails and text messages concerning a second date, which you have absolutely no intention of going on.

Think of it this way. If the table was turned and you were interested in a date, only to find out that they'd been faking interest in you, you probably feel embarrassed and humiliated.

If you're not interested in a date at least have the decency to be honest about your feelings with your date. If you want to end a relationship on an amicably note it's especially important that you are honest about your feelings.

If you're worried about hurting your dates feelings remember that while the truth might cause them a little pain now, the longer you take to be honest with them, the more painful the experience is likely to be for them.

If you're truly interested in your date, this question will let them know that you're interested in them, without being too subtle or too forward. This question is a fun flirty way of securing a second date.

This question should also reveal how your date feels that the date is going. If your date gives you an answer that signals that they are keen for another date, you're in luck. If your date tries to ignore or blow the question off then mentally move on.

After all the saying is true, there are plenty of fish in the sea. At least by asking your date this question you won't have to keep wondering whether or not they are interested in you.

Also it's true the more you practice doing something, the more skilled you become. So while it may be nerve wracking asking this question or just asking for a second date in general.

The only way it's going to get easier, is if you practice.

31. What is the funniest pick-up line that you've heard?

Once again this question is a great question to ask if you'd like to share a laugh with your date. After all the worse the pick-up line is, the funnier it is.

Perhaps your date will have a cheesy pick up line story that will leave you wondering why on earth anyone would use such a lame pick up line.

Sometimes things are also funnier in hindsight and while your date may not have been impressed back when someone tried to use a cheesy pick up line on them, they will probably be able to laugh at it in hindsight.

By asking this question you can also leave a mental note to yourself not to use the pick-up line your date mentioned, as obviously it's not very successful.

A word to the wise, refrain from ever using pick-up lines as they typically give people the impression that you use them often and are just interested in having one night stands.

No one ever takes someone who uses pick-up lines seriously. After all how many couples do you know who started dating after the person used a pick up line on the other?

You and your date don't have to limit your pick up line stories to events that occurred to you personally. If you've heard a funny pick up line in a movie or on television, feel free to share it with your date too.

Perhaps they might have even seen the same movie or television program. In which case you'll have something else in common and another topic to talk about.

Also considering turning this question into a game and seeing which of you can invent the cheesiest pick up line.

This game is guaranteed to provide a few laughs as you and your date alternate turns, each time trying to outdo each other with cheesy pick-up lines.

32. If you were Miss Universe, what advice would you give to aspiring beauty queens?

This question is important as your dates answer should give you an indication of what traits they value most in people, physical beauty, intellect, friendliness or social activism.

If your date gives advice that is beauty related, there is a chance that they're shallow and value physical beauty and looks over more important traits.

However, it's wise to first consider whether or not your date is joking, as they could well be mocking shallow pageant queens.

If however your date is serious you should rethink your relationship as it is never wise to date someone shallow as they might only like you for your looks and not your personality.

Shallow people also tend to be fickle and while your date may think you're beautiful one day, they may well change their mind the next day.

If your date answers shows that they care most about being a friendly and decent person this is a good sign, as they obviously have their priorities straight.

Perhaps your date has a secret aspiration to bring about positive change in the world. It's also important to note that friendly, kind people often make the best life partners, friends and parents.

If your date's answer gives you an indication that they value intellect above all other personality traits, whether or not this is a good or bad thing depends on your personality.

If you're a highly logical person yourself, you may be well-suited to a partner who prioritizes intellect above all else.

If you don't see yourself as an intellectual however, you may not be suited to date an obsessive intellectual as you might find their views on life pretentious and arrogant.

Although Miss Universe is always a female, feel free to ask this question to a male date, if you're female. A male date might laugh about this question, but that's just proof that they're having fun.

Chapter 5: Questions That Reveal Your Date's Passions and Interests

33. What is your dream job?

Your date's choice of dream job will reveal their aspirations and dreams. You can tell a lot about a person from their dream job.

As an example if your date's dream job is to become a famous actor or musician they probably want to be in the public eye and care about fame and fortune.

Whereas if your date's dream job is to run a charitable foundation, then they probably care most about helping other people than becoming famous or wealthy.

There is absolutely nothing wrong with someone aspiring to become either of these things, but you'll probably have a preference on whether you'd rather date an actor or a volunteer worker.

How big your date's dream is will also tell you whether they feel limited by constraints and obstacles or whether they are free to dream as big as they like.

If your date isn't afraid to aim for the stars they are more likely to be successful in accomplishing their dreams as to achieve your dreams you have to believe in yourself and take action.

It's ideal to date someone who dreams big as their passion will be infectious and may even inspire you to chase your dreams.

After all if you want to be successful the best thing you can do to reach your goals is to surround yourself with positive, passionate and successful people.

Those who are negative or too afraid to dream big won't support your dreams but will try and convince you that you're dreams are impossible to fulfil. If you can, try to avoid spending too much time with negative people.

34. What is the most important goal in your life?

Like some of the previous questions, this question should also give you a fair idea of what your date values and places great importance on.

You should be able to find out whether your date values their friends, family, their career or themselves most.

This question should also give you an idea of what life direction your date wants to take. Some life goals require a lot of sacrifice and dedication and this question will give you a sense of how much support your date might need from a long term partner.

As an example, if your date's most important life goal is to earn a Ph.D. in a given field, then they might need a partner who is patient enough to support them while they're at university studying for their doctorate degree.

If your date's goal is self-centered you may want to think twice about planning a second date with them.

After all wouldn't you rather date someone who cares about other people and will treat you like a King or Queen instead of their sidekick? Narcissistic people only care about themselves.

35. Have you figured out what your calling in life is?

If your date has figured out their purpose in life, they are likely to be passionate and driven.

Dating someone who is driven and motivated can be a great experience as their enthusiasm is bound to inspire you.

By giving your date an opportunity to talk about their biggest passion in life, their calling, you're giving them an opportunity to really talk about who they are and what they want to accomplish in life.

If your date answers that they haven't yet found their calling, that's okay too. After all not everyone is clear about what they want to do with their life and different people recognize their calling at different stages of life.

Some people will have their life planned out in exact detail as children or teenagers while others may find their calling during a midlife crisis or retirement.

You never know maybe your date will find their calling as a result of dating you. Sometimes life works in mysterious ways.

36. What is it like being your profession?

Most people enjoy talking about themselves, its human nature after all. The majority of people spend a sizeable portion of their week working and so they won't be short of things to talk about, should you happen to bring up the topic of their profession during casual conversation.

This is a great question to ask if you find a lull in the conversation. If you and your date work in different professions, you might even be able to teach each other a bit about what you do. Perhaps your date's occupation may be more interesting, than you first thought?

If you'd like you can also ask your date about some of their past jobs as you might find them interesting too.

You never know, perhaps your date worked as an extra on a big blockbuster film or worked as a part time model.

Perhaps you could even contemplate on asking your date about their very first job. Maybe they dressed up in a chicken suit as part of a job at a fast food restaurant. Or perhaps they had a really cushy first job working in a family member's office?

Just make sure not to ask your date about their job, after a long hard day at the office as they might want a well-deserved break from the stresses and demands of their job.

37. What is the best part of your job?

Although most people won't enjoy every aspect of their job, most people will have at least one aspect of their job that they genuinely enjoy.

As an example, some people thrive when they get to work in a team or interact with customers. While others may enjoy giving presentations or working with their hands.

By asking this question, you'll steer your conversation in a positive direction, by getting your date to talk about something they enjoy or are thankful for.

If you routinely ask positive questions, your date will begin to see you as a positive and fun person to be around. This is a great thing as positive people are more attractive than people who are negative or sarcastic.

If your date has nothing positive to say about their job, then their answer might be a warning sign that they are pessimistic and are not willing to take the initiative to look for a job where they might be happier.

After all it's unlikely that someone is forcing your date to remain in the same job. Slavery has been illegal for a long time now. If your date hates their job and doesn't look for a new job, the only person they have to blame is themselves.

38. What new hobby would you like to try?

Hobbies aren't only for children or teenagers. Adults who aren't afraid to pursue a new hobby are generally more successful in life. Why not ask your date about what new hobby they're keen to try out.

If your date laughs at this question, or remarks that hobbies are for children, alarm bells should ring. Never date someone who thinks they are too cool to participate in activities, as all they are proving is that they're too afraid to try new things and learn useful new skills.

If you're also interested in the hobby they bring up, why not arrange to try out the new hobby together. One of the reasons people don't try new hobbies is that they're afraid to put themselves in a situation where they don't know anyone.

As an example, if your date mentioned that they've always wanted to learn how to ballroom dance, but were too shy, offer to accompany them to a class.

Who knows you may even develop a passion for a hobby you've never considered before?

39. Do you like your job?

If your date tells you that they enjoy their job, this is a good sign as someone who is happy at work is more likely to come home in a good mood after work.

So many people who hate their job take out their frustration on their family members and friends.

The sad fact is that frustration and anger are contagious and if one person takes their anger out on their family the cycle will continue. Perhaps their child will retaliate by bullying someone at school. Or that their wife may lash out at her co-workers the next day.

If your date answers that they hate their job, then perhaps ask them what action they could take to make their job more enjoyable.

If your date takes your suggestion seriously, this is a good sign that they're willing to accept help and positive criticism.

If your date is puzzled by this question it may signal as they like to blame others like their boss or co-workers for their unhappiness, instead of taking responsibility and taking action to change the scenario.

Chapter 6: Questions to Get to Know Your Date on a Personal Level

40. What is the most courageous thing you've ever done?

Heroes don't only exist in superhero comics and movies. Everyday people from all walks of life commit courageous acts. Perhaps you're on a date with a hero and aren't yet aware of it.

This question is a great way to find out about your dates soft, caring side. Perhaps your date rescued a neighbour from a fire or stood up to a bully to protect someone who was incapable of defending themselves.

Each individual will also see different acts as courageous. Your dates answer will give you an indication of the type of acts that they personally see as courageous.

41. What is the most annoying thing someone has done to you?

Not only will this question provide a laugh, but it should also give you some insight into what your date's pet peeves are.

After all your date might choose one of your mannerisms or habits as something that annoys them. If this happens you probably shouldn't go on a second date with this person unless you really felt a connection with them.

You should never have to change the way you are to please a significant other. You deserve to be with someone who loves and accepts you, just the way you are.

42. What is your idea of a fun way to spend a day?

Be sure to listen up as your dates answer could give you a few ideas for future dates. If you do end up in a long term relationship, you could always make your dates suggestion come true.

After all there aren't many people in this world who wouldn't be impressed, if their partner remembered exactly what they told them on their first date.

The best way to let someone know that you care about them is to show them that you care about what they say and genuinely want them to be happy.

Also consider whether or not your date's idea of a fun day, matches with yours. As an example, if your date answers that they'd like to spend a day at the beach and you're not a fan of the beach, take note as perhaps you have contrasting personalities and are unlikely to enjoy the same activities.

However do bear in mind that just because you might not like your date's first suggestion of how to spend a day, doesn't mean that there won't be other activities and ways to spend a day that you both would enjoy.

43. What was the most influential life changing moment you've experienced?

This question is a little personal, so be sure not to ask this question straight away. Once you feel comfortable around your date, bring up this question to get to know your date better.

The reason why you should wait to ask this question is that some peoples most significant life changing moments are painful or negative.

As an example, your date may have been abused as a child or dumped by a long term partner and decided to turn their lives around.

If your date does reveal a particularly painful experience, make sure to keep the information they told you confidential. After all most sane people wouldn't forgive someone for spilling their biggest secrets.

If you maintain your date's trust, you'll demonstrate that your care about them and that you're a trustworthy and honorable person; two qualities many people specifically look for in a life partner.

However whether your dates life changing moment was spurred by a positive or negative event, by sharing this information with you, you'll likely share a bond afterwards.

Make sure that if your date answers this question, that you answer it in response too. After all you can't expect your date to open up to you, if you're like a closed book.

However don't fall into the trap of trying to compete with your date. Just because they told you about a painful or triumphant moment, doesn't mean you should try and top the moment they shared with you.

When it comes to sharing personal information, there is never a competition.

44. Would you ever date someone from a different religion?

Again you probably shouldn't ask this question too early on in a date. At least wait till you've been served your first course, if you're meeting your date in a café, coffee shop or restaurant.

This question is particularly important as if your date is from a different religion to you or holds different religious beliefs, they might not be willing to date you long term. It's preferable that you find this out sooner rather than later.

After all what's the point of dating someone for a few weeks or months and then finding out further down the track that they are unwilling to keep dating you, because of your religious beliefs.

On the flipside many people from varying religious denominations are willing to date someone with different beliefs, as long as they are able to respect each other's beliefs.

There are even happy couples in existence, where one partner is an atheist and the other a devout Christian. So if you're open minded try not to rule out dating someone who holds different religious beliefs.

Also keep in mind that even if your date shares your religious beliefs, it doesn't necessarily mean that you're compatible romantically as there are many more factors to take into consideration when dating someone.

As an example theoretically both you and your date could be Christian or Buddhist but could still disagree strongly when it comes to politics and government policies.

This is why you should never date someone simply because you share the same religious beliefs! Just because you share similar religious beliefs, or go to the same church doesn't mean you'll automatically live happily ever after.

Instead perhaps concentrate on finding a life partner who respects, loves and trusts you.

45. What are your friends like?

A person's friends are an important part of their lives. By asking about your date's friends you're showing that you're interested in meeting their friends and would never try to discourage them from spending time with their friends.

Unfortunately some girlfriends or boyfriends become quite possessive in a relationship and may even try to stop their significant other from spending time with their friends.

This isn't fair as people should never be expected to give up their friends for the sake of a relationship.

After all, why kick your friends to the curb for a new girlfriend or boyfriend, when you've probably known your friends far longer than your new partner?

If a date ever asks you to stop spending time with your friends, kick them to the curb instead as this behavior is beyond controlling.

Never let anyone tell you who you should or shouldn't spend time with. You're an adult and are capable of making your own decisions.

Besides if you're relationship doesn't work out, who will support you? That's right your friends and family. Never neglect your friendships for a date.

A date who really cares about your well-being would never ask you to choose between them and your friends anyway.

The way your date describes their friends will also give you an insight into what sort of person they are. After all most people are friends with people that they have things in common with.

This is because people, who share things in common, often find it easier to relate to each other and have more things to talk about.

Just think about how hard it would be to maintain a friendship with someone who enjoyed none of the activities or hobbies that you enjoy. It would be pretty tough, wouldn't it?

If your date describes their friends as crazy party animals, then there is a great chance that your date is also a crazy animal.

Or if your date describes their friends as hard working and loyal, there is also a significant chance that they too are hardworking and loyal. So listen carefully to the way your date describes their friends.

If on the rare chance your friend describes their friends in a negative light, perhaps be a bit concerned, as someone who doesn't think twice about bad mouthing their friends is also likely to bad mouth their family members and romantic partners.

Also try to envisage whether you could see yourself spending time with your date's friends. Do they sound like people you'd gladly socialize with? Would you mind spending Friday night at one of your date's friend's house?

Ask yourself whether or not you think you'd fit in with your date's friends. If you enter a long term relationship with your date, you'll be spending a lot of your free time with their friends.

Does your personality fit in with your date's friend's personalities? Or is your personality more likely to clash with your date's friends personalities.

As an example if your date's friends are loud party animals and you're a quiet homebody, your personalities might clash.

You'll also want to make a good impression, when you first meet your date's friends as most people look for dating advice from their close friends and will take their friend's opinion seriously.

In fact some people are even willing to dump a date that they feel a connection with, if their friends complain about their date.

Your date's friend's opinions will probably only come second to your date's family's opinion about you. Perhaps make a special effort to make a good first impression when meeting your date's best friend.

46. What was your childhood like?

By inquiring about your date's childhood you should also learn a great deal about their family.

You'll learn whether or not your date has siblings and whether or not they are particularly close with their immediate family members.

While some people spend much of their free time with their family, others only visit their close family members on special occasions such as Thanksgiving.

If your date grew up in another town, city, state or country to you, you'll also be able to swap stories as most likely you're experiences growing up will be vastly different. As peoples' experiences are greatly influenced by the area that they grew up in.

As an example if your date was brought up in another country, they are likely to have watched or played sports that aren't popular in your country.

So while a woman who was brought up in Australia may have played netball during her high school years, a woman who was brought up in America might have played volleyball or basketball instead.

If you're a family man or woman you'll probably want to date someone who is also close to their family. Not someone who only visits their family on the rare special occasion, such as Christmas.

After all you wouldn't want to date someone who would see visiting your family as a burden. You'd want to date someone who could easily fit into your family and would enjoy spending time with your family, just as much as you do.

Those who enjoy spending quality time with their family are also more likely to want to settle down one day and start a family of their own.

If you plan on being a parent one day, it's wise to choose a partner who already demonstrates how important family is to them.

If your date enjoys talking about their childhood there are many more related questions that you can ask them.

Perhaps ask them about the school they attended, their favorite games as a child and whether or not they had a pet growing up.

You could also consider asking your date about their favorite childhood memory.

47. Are you thrifty?

It's important for couples to share similar views on financial matters. After all if you're thrifty and your date isn't, they might find your cost saving techniques irritating.

If however you love to lead a comfortable lifestyle and enjoy the finer things in life you'd probably find it hard to date someone who is thrifty as you might see them as cheap.

A thrifty person and a spendaholic are likely to have daily disagreements, if they enter a relationship.

As an example, a thrifty person may insist on growing their own vegetables, while an ordinary person or a shopaholic would rather just buy their vegetables from the supermarket. As to them the hard work would far outweigh the benefits of having inexpensive fresh vegetables.

48. Who has been the greatest influence in your life?

This question should reveal the person whom your date sees as a role model and an inspiration. After all, although each person is a unique individual most people are influenced by others.

Perhaps your date sees a parent, grandparent, older sibling, teacher or a celebrity as the greatest influence in their life.

Once your date has revealed the person who has had the greatest influence on their life, perhaps ask them why that person has been so influential.

By asking this question you'll gain an insight into how your date has become the person they are today.

49. What should I know about you that I'd never think to ask?

This question is perhaps one of the best open ended questions you could ask.

By asking this question you give your date the opportunity to tell you something which they feel is important for you to know.

Sometimes people are so concerned with asking questions and getting answers that they forget to simply listen and give other people an opportunity to share information they feel is important, with them.

Who knows maybe your date will tell you something about themselves, which you might find surprising or fascinating.

Perhaps your date lived in multiple countries growing up, is a twin or has a secret talent.

50. What are some of your pet peeves?

Everyone has pet peeves. Some people are easily annoyed when someone leaves the toilet seat up or chews with their mouth open. By asking this question you'll get to know what annoys your date.

Hopefully your dates pet peeve is something reasonable as if your date picks something most people do as a pet peeve they are probably quite judgmental of other people.

An example of a normal justifiable pet peeve is if someone gets slightly annoyed when their flat mates or family members make a mess in the kitchen and leave it there, for them to clean up.

An example of a date that may have an unjustifiable pet peeve is someone who gets angry just because someone else holds a different opinion and disagrees with them on an issue. Unfortunately there are people who expect everyone to agree with all of their opinions.

In most cases those who are judgmental of others have an inflated ego and are hard to get on with as they constantly put other people down.

It's best to avoid dating people who are judgmental and have inflated egos as they'll always think that they know best and are unlikely to take any of your opinions seriously.

51. What's the riskiest thing you've ever done?

This question is a great way to find out whether your date takes wise or dangerous risks.

Ideally you should aim to date someone who takes calculated risks and never gambles with theirs or anyone else's life.

If you find out that you date has engaged in a potentially life threatening activity, you should think carefully about whether or not your date is likely to engage in such risky activities again.

As an example if your date tells you that they compete in illegal street car races or dare their friends to jump off bridges, steer clear as you date clearly has no regard for theirs or anyone else's life.

It's probably not a wise idea to date someone who has no regard for the law or their life, as there is a chance that they could get you into serious trouble.

52. How do you visualize your future?

How your date visualizes their future is extremely important, as their vision of the future should ideally match yours. Preferably after listening to your dates answer you'll also be able to imagine yourself as part of their future.

If the way you both visualize your futures doesn't match up, it doesn't necessarily mean you shouldn't go out on a second date together, as sometimes as people grow, their vision of their future changes and adapts.

However listen carefully as your dates answers may allude to some of their relationship deal breakers.

As an example, if they visualize a future with children and you aren't keen on having children, you may not be compatible with each other in the long run.

This question should also reveal some of your date's aspirations. Do they aspire to climb up the career ladder, build their own home or start investing?

53. What was the most important decision you've ever had to make?

This question may give you an insight into the obstacles and challenges that your date has had to overcome.

It's natural to feel as if sometimes you're the only one who has had to face countless hurdles; however, even those whose lives may look perfect face daily struggles.

This question allows you and your date to cut through the mundane small talk and you'll get to know who your date really is, not just the person they project to the world.

Also make sure to share your answer to this question with your date, as when two people share personal information they bond quicker.

Who knows, perhaps you and your date have overcome similar obstacles in your lives and will bond over your common experiences.

54. Do you have any enemies?

Hopefully your date either has no enemies, or just one or two enemies. While it's normal to have one or two enemies, who you find it impossible to get on with, it is unusual for one person to have several enemies.

If your date has several enemies, it could well be a warning sign that they are hard to get on with or hold grudges for long periods of time.

Beware, as a date that has lot of enemies is more likely to talk behind your back or act immaturely if you have a disagreement or break up.

55. Who is your hero?

Your date's choice of hero should tell you who they look up to and aspire to be more like. It is likely that your date has chosen their hero because of their hero's unique attributes.

Perhaps your date admires the work ethic of their favorite athlete or the selflessness of a person who puts others needs before their own.

Your date's choice of hero is important as it gives you an indication of who they want to become. In fact many people actually model their lives on their heroes' life.

If your date has a hero and they aren't a family member or close friend be sure to ask your date whether or not they've had the pleasure of meeting their hero.

If your date has met their hero, they'll probably have an exciting story to share with you. Who knows, perhaps their hero is someone famous?

If your date doesn't have a hero, don't worry as perhaps they are simply concerned with becoming the best version of themselves that they can be.

As long as your date is inspired and motivated, you shouldn't be concerned.

56. Which of your family members do you spend the most time with?

Firstly this is another great question to figure out whether or not your date is close to their family. However this question is extremely important as it will reveal which of your date's family members they are closest with.

If further down the track you enter into a long term relationship with your date, this is the family member who you'll have to impress and make a good first impression with.

If your date is particularly close with a family member they are likely to get their family members approval on any new girlfriends or boyfriends.

57. What is one thing that you couldn't live without?

This question will really test your date and reveal what it is that they truly value. If your date chooses a family member, pet or object that was gifted to them from a loved one, you should be rest assured that your date has their priorities in the right place.

However if your date chooses an expensive material object, which isn't a gift from a loved one, you should be concerned.

After all if you continued to date this person, they may well choose a material object like a watch or an expensive set of golf clubs, over you in the event of a fire.

There is no point dating someone who is likely to be more attached to an inanimate object than they are to you.

Don't settle for someone who values things above people, no matter how good looking they are.

58. Do you believe in God or in a Higher Power?

If you're particularly religious this question is a great answer to find out whether or not your date shares your belief in God.

This question may prompt further discussion as your date may not believe in a traditional Christian, Jewish or Muslim God, but may still believe in a God.

After all you don't have to be religious to believe in a God. Some people believe in a God, but disagree with some of the teaching of traditional religions. Everyone is entitled to form their own religious and spiritual beliefs.

Respecting someone else's religious beliefs doesn't mean that you have to accept them as fact, but that you agree to disagree and allow other people to form and keep their own opinions.

If you're religious and your date is an atheist, or vice versa you may want to talk further about your beliefs and how important they are to you.

If both you and your date have varying spiritual beliefs but can agree to respect each other's beliefs, there may well be hope for a relationship.

59. What is your biggest regret?

We all have regrets, it's impossible to live life without making mistakes now and then. However some regrets are bigger than others.

This question is a great way of finding out what your date could change about their life, if they could.

Perhaps your date betrayed one of their closest friends, cheated on a test or failed to take up the opportunity of a lifetime.

The great thing about this question is that it doesn't have to be a negative question. You could perhaps follow it up by encouraging your date and letting them know that we learn more from our mistakes than our triumphs and that in some cases it's never too late to turn things around and right your wrongs.

60. If you could start your life over, how would you do things differently?

This question should give you an indication of how happy your date is with their life.

People who are confident in themselves will answer that they wouldn't change anything or would just make a few changes, while those who aren't happy with their lives would talk about drastic changes they would make.

The fact of the matter is that no matter how badly you want to wind back the clock, it's not going to happen. So accept your mistakes as part of a learning curve and move on.

After all people learn much more and develop more as a person from their mistakes than they do from their successes.

We're all human and even the world's most successful people have failed. In fact successful people normally face failure and rejection on a regular basis.

Success is a simple numbers game, the more times you try something or face rejection, the more times you'll end up succeeding and meeting your goals.

This piece of advice applies to dating too. The more times you face rejection and start asking people you're interested out, the more chance you have of finding the love of your life.

If you're looking for love, go out on as many dates as you can until you meet the right person. If you don't share chemistry with the first person you go out on a date with, don't despair or get discouraged as the saying is true, there are plenty of fish in the sea.

After all you'll never find Mr. or Ms. Right by staying at home and expecting them to knock on your doorstep.

61. Are you a shopaholic?

If you're not a shopaholic you probably shouldn't date one as you may quickly become frustrated with the amount of money they spend on a whim.

If budgeting and keeping on top or your finances is important to you, definitely steer clear of extreme shopaholics as they may well have large credit card loans.

However if your date has a sizeable income and only spends what they can afford, their shopaholic tendencies shouldn't be cause for too much concern.

There is after all nothing inherently wrong with enjoying shopping, as long as you don't spend more than your disposable income.

62. Name one person from your past that you'd like to meet again?

This question should reveal the one person that your date wishes was still in their life.

Perhaps your date has lost contact with a childhood friend they'd like to reconnect with or would like to catch up with an extended family member who lives overseas?

If your date is able to name someone it shows that they value the relationships they have and want to make an effort to connect with the people who have touched their life.

After listening to your date's response, perhaps encourage them to try and get in contact with the person that they mentioned. With tools such as the internet and Facebook it's now easier than ever, to track down people from your past.

If however your date mentions that they'd love to reconnect with an ex from a previous relationship, alarm bells should ring in your head.

You should never date someone who talks about past relationships during a first date as your date may well still harbor feelings for their ex and may not be able to fully commit to a relationship with you.

You deserve to be with someone who is able to invest all of their romantic feelings in your relationship. After all, who wants to end up as someone's rebound guy or girl?

63. Who do you turn to for advice?

Firstly, this question should reveal whether or not your date has any close relationships. Not romantic relationships but close friendships or relationships with family members.

If your date doesn't have anyone that they can turn to for advice, they may well have an issue with letting people get close to them emotionally.

If this is the case beware that if you get into a long term relationship with this person, they may well become clingy, as you may be the only person that they feel they can confide in.

If you don't think you can handle being the only person your date can turn to, definitely think twice before requesting a second date.

Thinking carefully about this may save you and your date a lot of potential stress and heartbreak in the long run.

If your date does reveal that they have someone to turn to for advice, then you should be pleased that they are able to connect emotionally and form bonds with others.

Just make sure that the person they turn to for advice isn't their ex, as again you should never be the third wheel in your own relationship.

64. What is your first memory?

This question is a fun question to ask and may get your date thinking, as many people don't think about their oldest memories on a regular basis.

Perhaps your date's first memory dates back to when they visited Disneyland as a four year old? Or perhaps their first memory was of their first day of school? You'll never know unless you ask.

This question is bound to reveal some interesting personal stories. Perhaps you can even share your first memory, so that you can compare them with each other.

As an example, which of you can remember an event from a younger age?

65. Which personality trait, do you value most in others?

Like some of the previous questions, this question should reveal what your date values and places importance on.

This question should give you a fair indication of what sort of people your date is likely to get on well with.

It's also an opportunity to gain an insight into what personality traits your date may want their life partner to have. As an example, if your date answers that they value passion as a trait, they'll probably be instantly attracted to people who are passionate.

When your date answers, think carefully about whether or not, you yourself display this trait.

As an example, if your date mentions that they value honesty and you don't think you're a particularly honest person, you may not be well-matched as potential partners.

66. Which personality trait, do you find the most irritating in others?

This question is a subtle way to ask your date about the personality traits and habits that they don't want a potential partner to display.

After all how many people are brave enough to ask their date "what personality traits do you think make people unattractive"?

If you find that you display the trait, which your date finds irritating, you may well want to question whether or not you and your date should continue dating.

After all, you shouldn't have to change to please your date and you certainly shouldn't have to feel as if you're tip toeing around your date in an effort not to annoy them.

Your ideal life partner would love you regardless of any slightly annoying personality traits you might display.

Chapter 7: Questions That Reveal Your Date's Thoughts about Relationships.

67. What do you think is the biggest mistake couples make in a relationship?

This question should inform you on how your date thinks a relationship should function.

Perhaps your date thinks most couples don't make an effort to spend enough quality time together, or perhaps they think most couples let go of their appearance after they've been in a committed relationship for a few months.

Ideally you should agree with your date's answer, if you don't see it as a mistake that couples make, you probably have contrasting views on what makes a successful relationship.

68. Describe your ideal relationship?

This question could be one of the most important questions you could ask a date. After all people are individuals and all have a different notion on what makes an ideal relationship work.

As an example, some people prefer relationships in which one person is the bread winner, while the other is a home maker who tends to the house and the children.

This situation may work for some couples but would be less than ideal for a couple made up of two people who are both passionate about climbing their respective career ladders.

If you're female and envisage a life as a home maker or as a career woman it's important to let your date know about your view.

After all there is no point wasting a few months in a relationship only to find out that your partner expects you to quit your job once you get married, if you're passionate about your career.

If you're male it's also important to try and find out your partners expectations for a relationship. If you're not willing to take on the burden of being the sole bread winner in a relationship, you won't be well-matched with a woman who wants to be a housewife.

69. What are you looking for in a relationship?

This is a basic fundamental question which every dater should ask on their first date. It's wise to find out exactly why your date is interested in getting into a relationship.

Perhaps your date is looking to find the love of their life and settle down or just wants a casual relationship with no strings attached.

There is no circumstance under which someone who wants a causal one night stand and someone who wants to settle down should begin dating. Such a relationship would be doomed to fail.

However if you don't ask this question, you'll be left in the dark and may not be on the same page as your date.

This is actually a great question to ask on a first date as it's a great way to ensure that both you and your date are looking for the same type of relationship. Open communication is an essential ingredient for a successful relationship.

As an example, many men and women complain that their date cheated on them, when they failed to communicate the terms of their relationship with their partner. Perhaps their partner never had anything in mind other than a fling or a causal short term relationship.

To spare yourself heartbreak make sure that your date is interested in the same sort of relationship you are.

If they aren't, simply walk away as no matter how attractive or charming they are, a relationship between the two of you would likely disintegrate.

If you're looking for a casual relationship, don't tip toe around the fact. It's only fair to let your date know.

If however you're looking for a committed long term relationship, it's also best to let your date know this as soon as possible. Preferably sometime on your first date together.

70. How many times have you had your heart broken?

How many times a person has had their heart broken can tell you a lot about them. If your date has had their heart broken a dozen times, it's safe to say that they fall in love easily.

If your date admits that they've indeed been heartbroken a dozen times, you should be concerned as they may well be the type of person who falls in and out of love easily.

Wouldn't you rather be in a relationship with someone who falls in love with you because you're special and unique? Not because they fall in love with anyone who is willing to date them?

If your date has only been heartbroken once or twice before you can be rest assured that they take relationships seriously and will invest their whole heart into a potential relationship with you.

If your date reveals that they are still recovering after a messy break up, you have to consider whether or not you're willing to comfort them and work at getting them to let you get close emotionally.

71. What scares you the most about entering a new relationship?

It's natural to have fears about entering a new relationship.

The trouble is that most people are unwilling to share these fears with their new partner and so their fears grow larger. This doesn't have to be the case.

If you share your fears with a potential partner, early on in a relationship you'll be able to confront these fears and work on them together.

You might even find out that your date shares similar fears or that your fears are unfounded. If you fears are unfounded you may even be able to share a laugh about them with your date.

Some fears seem so serious in your own mind, but when you share them out loud you find out that they're just plain silly.

72. Why did you agree to come on a date with me?

So often people ponder what it is that their date or partner sees in them.

Stop pondering and simply ask your date what it is about you that made them ask you out or agree to come on a date with you. They are bound to come up with at least a few reasons why.

If your date in turn asks you what made you decide to go on a date with them, be honest. Don't be afraid to tell them that you like their smile, that you enjoy your conversations with them or that you find them attractive.

A compliment is sure to put a smile on your dates face and break the ice. After all it's incredibly hard not to like someone who compliments you.

73. If you were to ask me on a second date, where would we go?

Firstly only ask this question if you're keen on spending more time with your date.

If you're not interested, don't fake any interest as it is unfair on your date, who may well be developing unrequited feelings for you.

This question is also a great way of seeing whether or not your date is enjoying themselves and is still interested in you. If your date is slow to respond or looks awkward about answering the question they might not be that interested in a second date with you.

If your date has a smile on their face and quickly comes up with an answer, they may well be trying to impress you. If this is the case a second date together may well be in the cards.

If your date's suggestion of a second date sounds like your idea of a good time why not ask them what day would suit them?

74. What is the worst thing that could happen on a first date?

On a first date you don't want all your questions to be too serious. This question is a fun question and chances are whatever your date says, won't actually happen on your date together.

If your date has a keen sense of humor, why not brainstorm a list of the top ten worst things that could happen on a first date? If you're out on a date at a coffee shop, café or restaurant why not get out a pen and write the list down on a napkin.

If the date goes well you can write a cute message on the other side of the napkin and give it to your date to keep as a memento of your first date.

An example of something you could write on the other side of the napkin is "Since none of these things happened I declare this date a success", along with your phone number.

75. What is the longest relationship you've been in?

If you're looking for a long term relationship, you'll want to hear that your date has been in previous long term relationships, as those who have been in a long term relationship are more likely to want to enter a committed long term relationship again.

If your date is someone who jumps quickly from one relationship to another and you're looking for a committed long term relationship you should take into the fact that you're date hasn't been in a long term relationship into consideration.

You shouldn't immediately rule your date out, but weigh up this information against all the other factors such as your chemistry and their personality.

76. Do you generally follow your head or your heart?

Some people follow their head and logic, while others primarily follow their heart and intuition. By asking your date this question you may begin to understand the way they think.

Ideally you should date someone who shares a similar opinion with you on this question.

However sometimes couples that have one partner who follows their head and one partner that follows their heart are successful as they are more balanced as each partner's strengths are the other partner's weaknesses.

77. Do you think the past matters, in a relationship?

This question is important because if your date doesn't think the past matters in a relationship they may be more likely to commit adulterous acts or treat you badly as they show no responsibility over their actions.

Yes, it's important not to dwell on the past and to live in the present but you should always remember that people have to live with the consequences of their past actions.

78. How and when would you know that I'm the right one?

Most people spend their life looking for the one person that they feel they are compatible with.

By asking this question you'll get to understand what your date is looking for in a long term partner or a future wife or husband.

Don't be surprised however if your date tells you that they don't have a time line on how long it should take to know if someone is the one.

Normally people just have a gut feeling, which lets them know that their significant other is the person they'd like to share the rest of their life with.

If your date responds in this way, perhaps ask them how long it normally takes them to decide whether or not a relationship has a future.

79. If your parents don't approve of me, how will you react?

Most people are extremely close with their family. So the way in which your date's family reacts to you is of great importance.

Of course you can give yourself the best shot possible on creating a positive first impression by following a few simple rules.

Dress appropriately in a tidy outfit, greet each member of your date's family warmly and take a small gift such as a bottle of wine or a box of chocolates with you as a gift to your date's parents.

However no matter how hard you try to impress your date's family, there is no guarantee that they will like you.

Most importantly though, just be yourself. People's families are adept at telling whether or not a date is being honest and truthful or fake.

This question is a great way of finding out how your date is likely to respond to a scenario where their parents or other family members don't approve of your relationship.

The best answer possible would be that your date would stand up for you while still respecting their family.

If you get the impression that your date would dump you because their parents didn't like you, move on.

Someone who isn't brave enough to stick up to their parents and defend their partner doesn't have control over their own life and is likely to look to their parents for advice on every single aspect of their life.

When you date someone you are meant to be their key support system and the person they turn to first for an opinion.

80. If you were guaranteed not to be caught, would you cheat on your partner?

Sadly statistics show that over half of people in committed relationships would cheat on the love of their life, if they were guaranteed not to get caught.

In fact around half of those in committed relationships have already cheated on their significant other.

This question will reveal how faithful your date is likely to be in a relationship. If cheating is a deal breaker for you do not go on a date with someone who admits that they would cheat, providing that they wouldn't be caught.

Someone who is dedicated to your relationship and really is in love with you would never dream of cheating on you. Yes, perhaps they might take a quick second glance at an attractive man or woman, but they wouldn't go any further.

Also beware that those who cheat on their partners are also more likely to do things that they shouldn't. A cheater is likely to cheat on an exam or steal credit for someone's work in the office place.

81. What is more important to you, your career or personal life?

Unless your career is the most important thing in your life, you probably don't want to go out with someone who places their career first.

After all if your date chooses their career as their response to this question they are likely to work long hours and have little time left to spend with you.

If you're date has little time to spend with you, they really shouldn't be dating you, or anyone else for that matter.

Ideally people should only date if they are willing and able to invest a decent amount of time and energy into making their relationship work.

All successful relationships require that each person makes an effort to spend time with their significant other. This is why so many long distance relationships flop within the first few months. For a relationship to succeed both partners need to make it a priority.

If you've always dreamed of having children, this question will be of even more relevance as a person who puts their career ahead of their relationship, will also put their career ahead of their children.

Yes, having a partner that is able to contribute a great deal financially to the household is helpful, but a partner who spends more time with you is far more valuable than a partner who works all day and provides a great salary, but never spends time with you.

The famous saying "money can't buy you happiness" has some truth to it. Money can't buy you happiness in the long run and only provides temporary fulfillment.

As an example, if a wealthy person buys a flashy new sports car, in all likelihood they'll only be happy for a few days. Once their neighbor buys a newer or flasher model, they'll start lusting over an even more expensive car.

Sadly most people don't realize that buying a new car isn't as important as cherishing your relationships, both romantic and platonic.

82. Do you see a future with me?

While this question is a great question to ask, make sure not to ask it on the first few dates as you may scare you date off by getting too serious too quickly.

Perhaps only ask this question once you have started to consider a future with your date.

If your date does see a future with you, take this as a huge compliment as obviously your date has strong feelings about you and is already envisaging a future with you.

If your date answers that they haven't considered a future with you or wouldn't consider a future with you, your relationship should end there.

There is no point wasting your time with someone who isn't serious about you, unless you're not looking for a long term relationship.

83. If you met the right person, would you be ready to settle down?

If you're looking to find the man or woman of your dreams and settle down together you'll want to date someone who is willing and able to give up single life and commit to one person.

Not all people are ready to commit to a long term relationship. In fact some people in their late forties or fifties still haven't reached a stage where they are willing to settle down.

If your date answers that they're not ready to settle down, perhaps ask them why that is. Perhaps they are a free spirit and don't want to be tied down to one person or one location.

Or perhaps there are still a lot of individual goals that they want to accomplish before settling down, getting married or starting a family.

Whatever their reasoning is, if someone isn't ready to settle down, don't force them to. You'll only end up regretting it further down the road when they disappear from your life without a goodbye.

84. What is the biggest mistake that someone could make on a first date?

When you ask this question, have your fingers crossed that you haven't made the mistake that your date answers.

Although only a rude date would actually answer with something you've done on your date. So don't worry too much.

Like some of the previous questions, this question should get a laugh out of your date. Or your date might answer this question seriously and then you'll get to know what their worst case scenario is.

Most likely it's something you couldn't do on a date if you tried. As an example perhaps the worst mistake someone could make on a first date would be not to listen and to talk nonstop for the entire date.

85. Why did your last relationship end?

This could be a touchy subject, so make sure not to ask this question until you've gotten to know your date well enough.

Hopefully your date's last relationship ended amicably, as you don't want to date someone who will hold a grudge against you, if your relationship doesn't work out.

After all you don't want to date someone who would spread lies or gossip about you if you were to break-up.

Some people have the habit of becoming quite two faced, when they are displeased or angry with someone they are close to.

If your date's last relationship ended amicably it is also a sign that they are mature and responsible. Two qualities that you should look for in a potential life partner.

If your date's last relationship ended on a sour note, try to find out why. In some cases your date might not be at fault and may have been victim to an unhealthy relationship.

On the other hand also make sure that the relationship didn't end badly because of something they did as history has a habit of repeating itself and if they ruined one relationship they might ruin another one.

86. What do you think is the most important thing in a relationship?

This question should be a rather simple and straightforward question to answer.

Hopefully your date will answer that love is the most important thing in a relationship. Other good possible answers include passion, children, loyalty and friendship.

If your date answers that money or sex is the most important thing, you should run for the hills. Seriously, your date shouldn't answer with a materialistic or sexual answer.

87. Which is more important to you money or a relationship?

This is another question which is designed to reveal whether your date values money or material items, more than their romantic partners and relationships.

If your date answers that money is more important than a relationship, then hopefully they are trying to be funny and are joking. If however you think their answer is serious, end the relationship right there and then.

Money is important and allows people to pursue their dreams and provide a comfortable lifestyle for themselves and their family.

However money is not the be all and end all and if you rely on money to make you happy, you'll never be satisfied with what you have.

If your date values money more than people then they are destined to become unhappy. You deserve better than to be in a relationship with someone who is bitter, obsessed with money or depressed.

88. If your partner cheated on you, what would you do?

Just because a large percentage of the world cheats on their partners, doesn't mean it's right.

Ideally your partner will answer that they wouldn't put up with someone cheating on them and would leave the relationship.

If your date claims that they would leave the relationship, it shows that they have standards and are not so insecure that they would be a door mat for their partner.

Those who won't put up with cheating are also far less likely to cheat on a partner themselves, as they have higher moral standards than most people who cheat on their partner.

If your date answers that they would try to forgive their partners, this may be ok, as long as they only put up with their partner cheating once.

Yes, it's perfectly fine to attend couples counseling sessions in a bid to save a marriage but no one should ever stay in a relationship after they've been cheated on twice.

To do so would be incredibly naïve and sends out a message that you'll put up with being treated badly. After all people only treat you, the way you let them. If you're clear that you're unwilling to put up with cheating, there is less chance that you'll be cheated on.

89. Do you ever see yourself getting married?

While some people grow up envisaging their wedding day, others are adamant that they'll never get married.

While some people do end up changing their mind, either way, you shouldn't count on it and should try to find out whether your date plans on getting married or not.

If getting married is important to you, then this question will be particularly important as you'll want to make sure that your date also dreams of getting married one day, before taking your relationship to the next level.

If your date answers that they would like to get married, perhaps ask them how they envisage their dream wedding. Perhaps you could play a little game together and make up a dream wedding together.

This is a fun exercise as there are so many possibilities. Would you elope or have a traditional white wedding? What sort of music would play at your reception?

Chapter 8: Questions That Reveal Your Date's Thoughts on Family and Marriage

90. Would you like to have kids one day?

Again this is probably not the best question to ask early on in a relationship.

However after a few weeks of dating you may want to consider asking this question. As for many people the decision whether or not to have children is a relationship deal breaker.

Some people grow up researching probably names for their future children while others are adamant that they'll never have children.

Do take your date's answer seriously if they tell you they don't want children. Many people who want children find it extremely difficult to understand that there are others who have no interest in having children or who don't even like being around children.

A word of advice, never tell someone who doesn't want children, that they'll change their mind as they'll find your comment patronizing.

After all some people aren't destined to become parents but make wonderful aunties, uncles and older siblings.

After all there is more than one way of contributing to a child's upbringing and you don't need to become a parent to inspire and nurture a child.

If however your date answers that they'd like to have children, go ahead and ask them about how many they would ideally like.

After all if you and your date both want children in the future, it doesn't necessarily mean that you'll be compatible as one of you may want more children than the other.

As an example if you want one or two children and your date wants five or six, you may have a potential problem, a problem, which you might not be able to compromise on.

91. What is your family like?

A person's family is one of the most influential forces in their life. Even those who aren't close to their family or are estranged from their family are likely to have been influenced by their family members.

So a great way to get to know your date better is to get to know their family. Play close attention to the information your date tells you about their family because if your relationship becomes serious you'll most probably get to meet the family members, your date tells you about.

This question is also a great open ended question which lends itself to further discussion. If you're lucky your date may also share some funny family stories with you or perhaps stories from their childhood.

92. What is your father like?

Your date's father will have had a great influence on them, if of course they were lucky enough to grow up with a father in their life.

If your date answers that they never got the opportunity to meet their father, or that their father passed away, it is of extreme importance that you display empathy before asking about what their mother is like.

If your date grew up without a father his or her mother is probably the biggest influence in their life.

If however your date does talk about their father, perhaps encourage them to share some of their favorite memories of times that they spent with their father.

93. What is your mother like?

Like your date's father their mother is likely to have been a huge influence on their life. Chances are that your date is a little like their mother, personality wise.

In fact as a follow up question you could ask your date about the personality traits or mannerisms that they've picked up from their mother.

If your date reveals that they are close to their mother, perhaps ask them to share some of their favorite memories of times that they shared with their mother.

94. What does your family do when you spend time together?

Of course use discretion when it comes to asking this question. Don't ask this question if you've already found out that your date isn't close to their family or is estranged from their family.

If your date does have a healthy relationship with their family members, this question is a great way to gain insight into your date's family.

Hopefully the activities your date lists appeal to you as if you enter a long term relationship with your date, you're likely to spend a lot of time with his or her family.

Also be sure to ask your date about their favorite family activity. Perhaps their family goes skiing together every winter or plays board games once a week. Your date's answer might surprise you.

For a laugh perhaps have a little contest where you and your date compete to see who can come up with the dorkiest family activity or ritual.

By revealing the embarrassing side of your family, you'll show your date that you're comfortable around them.

Your date will also get the impression that you don't try too hard to impress other people and care more about those that you love, than what other people might think.

Also be sure to share information about what your family does when they are together, with your date. Your date is bound to be just as interested in your family as you are with theirs.

After all if your date is particularly interested in you, they'll be keen to gain hints on how they might be able to make a good first impression on your family members.

So also feel free to give your date some hints on how they can win your family over. That is if you're genuinely interested in your date.

As an example, if your father enjoys talking about a particular sport, let your date know so that they start a conversation about it with your father.

As another example, if your mother enjoys playing cards, don't forget to tell your date as they might remember and bring over a pack of cards to play with your mother in the future.

Or if your sister is a chocoholic perhaps mention it as your date may remember to purchase a box of chocolates to give to your sister upon meeting her.

If you can think of any common activities which your families share, keep them in mind, if your relationship becomes serious further down the track you may be able to introduce your families to each other.

As an example, if you've mentioned that your families enjoy Italian cuisine you could arrange for your families to meet for dinner at a local Italian restaurant in the future.

95. Are you the only, youngest, middle or oldest child in your family?

Some people argue that birth order determines many of peoples' personality traits. So why not ask your date about their birth order?

Also be sure to ask your date about the advantages and disadvantages of being the oldest, youngest, middle or only child in their family.

If your date is the youngest in their family they may well have been given extra attention growing up by their parents.

Although there are disadvantages of being the youngest in a family, perhaps your date was always stuck wearing their older siblings' hand me downs.

If your date is the middle child in their family they may well have a competitive streak, which they may have developed in an effort to get their parents attention and to step out of their older siblings shadows.

As the oldest sibling is typically the first to graduate high school, go to university and get a job. However there are some slight disadvantages to dating someone who is the eldest of their singling. As an example, the eldest child in a family is often fiercely independent and may find it difficult to let you in emotionally.

If your date is an only child perhaps ask them about what it's like to grow up without any brothers or sisters.

Perhaps you can also ask them about how they managed to entertain themselves or if they were close to their cousins or extended family members.

One plus side to dating an only child is that they are usually very creative, as they may have developed a great imagination as a result of entertaining themselves as a child.

96. Would you ever consider adopting a child?

While some people can't imagine not giving birth to their own children, others can't imagine having their own biological children, when there are already so many children in the world who are in need of a loving home.

This question should reveal whether or not your date would ever consider adopting a child.

If you're unable to conceive your own child or have always wanted to adopt a child, this question will be particularly relevant, as in the long term you wouldn't want to date someone who is close-minded about adoption.

If your date is open-minded about adoption perhaps ask them whether or not they have a preference about domestic or international adoption.

Unfortunately, although most countries have thousands of orphans, western countries often have laws and regulations in place which protect birth parents right to their child and make adoption extremely difficult.

This is why many couples choose to adopt a baby or child from a foreign country.

97. Are you willing to become a stay at home parent?

Please use caution when it comes to asking this question.

If you're male, make sure not to ask this question in a way that implies that you'd prefer or expect your life partner to be a stay home parent.

Many modern women would be highly offended if their boyfriend or partner were to assume that she should stay at home, while he works as a breadwinner.

If you're a career-minded female and don't think your partner will be offended, why not ask your date how he feels about a scenario in which he would be a stay at home father?

If your date laughs at this question or doesn't take it seriously perhaps consider whether or not your date has old fashioned sexist tendencies.

The reality is that both men and women make great stay at home parents. Whether a parent makes a good stay at home parent, doesn't have anything to do with their gender but their personality.

This question may also bring up the discussion about whether or not your date believes a parent should stay home at all to take care of the children. As in many families young children are taken care of by other family members or are put into daycare.

98. At what age do you see yourself getting married and settling down?

Only ask this question if you've already asked the previous questions about your date's views on marriage and settling down.

If your date has already mentioned that they would like to get married and settle down, this question is a great way of getting them to open up on their rough time line.

This question is important as it will give you and your date a fair idea of whether or not your rough time frames are compatible.

After all if you plan to get married in your mid to late twenties and your date doesn't want to settle down and get married until their mid-thirties to early forties, your life plans may not be compatible.

Just because you and your date may have different ideas on when you'd like to get married and settle down doesn't mean you should end your relationship as people change and you may well be able to compromise.

99. What are some of the things you want to accomplish before getting married?

Hopefully your date will have a few answers to this question. Sadly so many people give up their childhood dreams upon becoming adults, in order to get married or settle down.

The reality is that unless you've found the love of your life, you should never be in a rush to get married. No matter what age you are.

Never give in to society's message that you're not complete without a significant other. You are a complete person, with or without a significant other.

Remember that a single person is far happier than a person who is in an unhappy relationship. Being in a relationship doesn't automatically guarantee that you'll be happy.

If you're still young, why not concentrate on fulfilling a few of your childhood dreams before you settle down and have a family? If your date truly cares about you, they'll wait.

If they're too impatient then be thankful that you discovered that they aren't the right person for you, before it was too late.

After all you don't want to marry your significant other, only to find out that they're unwilling to support you in achieving your goals.

Although it's still possible to achieve your dreams once you're married or have children, it becomes a lot harder as you have more responsibilities and other people to take into consideration.

Also make sure to share some of your personal goals that you plan to accomplish before getting married. If your date is supportive they'll be inspired and not be put off by your ambition.

99. Would you marry someone who comes from a different background or social status?

Although most western countries no longer have rigid classes, unfortunately a large proportion of people are still influenced by power, money and status.

By asking your date about whether or not they are open to dating and marrying someone from a different background or social status, you'll find out how important image, power, money and status are to your date.

If you're a liberal, modern person you'll most likely be better off dating someone who is open minded when it comes to things such as backgrounds, than someone who holds on to rigid old fashioned ideals.

If you're lucky enough to be raised by a wealthy family or have accumulated your own wealth, you might find this question particularly useful as it could potentially weed out dates who are only interested in dating you for your money or social standing.

100. Do you believe that divorce is a valid option for those in unhappy marriages?

While some people are traditionalists and believe marriage should be a lifelong commitment, other people believe that an unhappy married couple should be permitted to get a divorce, rather than remain in a loveless marriage.

This question is particularly important if you plan to get married in the future, as if there is a chance that you and your date will settle down together, you'll need to talk about what the commitment of marriage means to the two of you.

For some couples divorce is not an option and marriage isn't entered into lightly. If your date doesn't believe in divorce and you do, you'll have to seriously consider whether or not you can even imagine yourself marrying your date in the future.

If you don't think you can commit to a lifelong marriage, make sure you let your date know this as it might be one of their relationship deal breakers.

After all it's not fair of you to keep dating them if there is no chance of your relationship developing into a lifelong partnership.

Remember that even if you do personally believe in the option of the divorce, divorce should never be your first option.

All long term relationships go through their ups and downs and you should always try to work out your problems, before giving up on a marriage, or a long term relationship for that matter.

If in the future you find yourself in a long term relationship or marriage, perhaps consider counseling sessions if you hit rough periods in your relationship.

Counseling is a great marriage or relationship tool, as sometimes couples get so angry at each other, that they can no longer remember what it was that they were originally fighting about.

A counselor is trained to be objective and impartial and will try their best to get couples to communicate openly about their feelings.

101. What are some things that married couples can do to keep their relationships fresh and exciting?

Unfortunately so many married couples take their partner for granted and no longer make an effort to keep the spark in their relationship alive.

When the spark in a relationship is no longer present it's easier for couples to fall out of love or to argue frequently.

The great news is that even if the spark in a couple's relationship has been extinguished, it can easily be reignited with some effort.

This question is important as it will show you whether or not your date will be likely to make an effort, should you continue to date and perhaps even get married one day.

If you're date put forwards at least a few creative ideas of things that couples can do to keep their relationship fresh, rest assured that they would probably make a committed life partner or spouse.

If your date doesn't come up with any suggestions, you should be slightly concerned as if your date can't come up with any suggestions now, to impress a new date, how much effort are they going to make after they've been in a marriage for twenty years?

There are countless things a couple can do to put a spark back into their relationship. These changes don't have to be huge or significant.

As an example a couple could make a conscious decision to schedule date nights each week. Another idea could be for a couple to take a vacation out of their home city, each year to celebrate the anniversary of their marriage.

Made in the USA
Middletown, DE
12 June 2017